Dying
to Live

A Guide to Living
with Motor Neurone Disease

KEVIN JORDAN

Contents

About this Book 1

The Fall 4
Carla 11
Sidelines 17
Looking Back 21
Nothing to Lose 28
Rugby and Me 33
Hello My Love 38
Choices 41
Looking Inward 46
Keeping the Glass Half Full 50
Laura and John 57
Luke 60
Trevor 62
Susan 65
Alan 68
Making a Difference 70
Looking Forward 73
Reflections 77

Links and References 98
About the Author 99

About this Book

Rae Nash

I met Kevin in 2012 through the *Sharp Pencils Creative Writers* Meetup group. He asked me to help him write a 'memoir' for his sons. He was 42 years old with three sons younger than 10 years old. He'd been diagnosed with Motor Neurone Disease (MND) and wasn't expected to live more than five years. And there began an extraordinary journey for both of us.

Initially we met weekly either at his office, and when he was no longer independent we met at his home. Kevin spoke, I recorded and transcribed each session as month by month a manuscript slowly emerged. Each meeting gave me a glimpse of the intense struggle being waged day by day. The anger, desperation and despair, his intimate companions, threatened to consume and overwhelm Kevin, and some days me too. My many years as a professional nursing sister gave me the empathy and fortitude to stay the course and participate in a small way in the unfolding of this 'memoir'.

Kevin felt most deeply the continued remorseless loss of independence that the condition imposes. His love and respect for Carla and the burden for her and those who have been part of his life was often the centre of our discussions; his inability to participate in being a husband and a dad.

Instead of seeing Kevin become a mournful, demanding, unhappy man, I have witnessed a man who has grown in strength, emotionally and spiritually. As each new challenge presented itself he has found the courage to accept. Often as I have listened to Kevin I know that I do not possess the courage he does; nor will I ever. I leave his home in awe of his determination, not only to live longer than the statistics suggest, but to do the living with joy and determination.

This book honours Kevin's life with MND; Carla his wife, his sons, Luke, Joel and Kian, and those he knows and loves, and who love him.

Those who have MND will know and understand and take courage from Kevin's way of dealing with a life for which he was not prepared. His indomitable spirit shines like a beacon.

Kevin in sharing your thoughts, feeling and strength with me, your journey has influenced mine in ways that are not easily put into words.

I am privileged to have been part of your journey.

Thank you Kevin.

The Fall

It had been a hectic week. I fell in the garage on Thursday after I had been to hydrotherapy. It happened as I got out of the car and tried to take the step up. I knew that if both my feet were in front of my hips I would fall backwards. Strange to have to be aware of something like that, but on this occasion the awareness did not save me from a fall. Had something changed?

Viv called an ambulance and by the time it had arrived Carla was with me. She drove behind the ambulance to Olivedale Clinic where I had stitches. They also sent me for x-rays and a CT brain scan to make sure that my head and my neck were okay. At the time I didn't feel anything emotionally. There seemed to be no damage. I was frustrated because I had to spend four hours in the emergency ward at Olivedale while they stitched me up and sent me for X-rays, but all seemed okay. Friday was fine too.

Then over the weekend I started thinking. The significance of having had a second serious fall dawned on me. My first fall had been on Boxing Day 2010. Carla and I had all the children with us, Luke, Joel, Kian and all the cousins. I'd fallen down the stairs in the amphitheatre at the Monte Casino Bird Park; I'd hit my head and blood was gushing from my right temple. We had sped to Fourways Hospital for stitching and the whole room had been splattered with blood by the time the doctor had finished.

Now I wondered whether I was deteriorating more quickly than I'd realized. How much more time did I have left? The evening before I had been on the verge of tears and eventually I did cry. I'd held it together till that point, but processing all the information about the future made me feel very sad. How much time do I still have to be able to walk, to speak, to act normally? Normal? Already I am not normal. I have to be fed. I have to have my bum wiped. All these thoughts churned in my mind. I felt so scared of the future. For the first time I had a genuine fear of what was to come.

Psychological factors have been the biggest issue, and I think I've managed them well. I continuously try to control my emotions of fear, sadness and loss but continuous emotional control is very difficult when you have to confront challenges of how to maintain your speech and mobility. My feelings about this were terrifying. Physical, tangible symptoms were far easier for me to accept. We needed a wheelchair, so we bought one. In the wheelchair, I was able to get about and I still had a certain level of independence.

Had something changed? I felt okay at the time of my fall, but four days later I didn't. At my next physiotherapy session I had to walk up and down stairs. I was absolutely desperate with fear. The adrenaline pumped through my veins and even though I managed, it took every ounce of my physical and mental strength to do it. When I went to speech therapy again we spoke about my speech and swallowing, which was still a hundred per cent.

I felt so much loss and sadness. I was afraid of my fear. It felt like being buried alive and not being able to get out. I dreaded not being able to do anything while I was fully aware that I was unable to move or do anything. Not being able to eat was not the biggest loss, but not being able to speak; not being able to convey my emotions and feelings and thoughts; not to be able to reach out and touch or snuggle or hug or kiss was heart-breaking. All those had to be done to and for me. I was sad because I could not move to be able to do things spontaneously with my sons, and Carla. I didn't find the fact of death scary – my getting to the point of death was. Had something changed?

Yes, it had. The fall had triggered my emotions and brought them to the surface so that I focused on myself more than I had been in the past. I thought: Is it wrong to ask more from others or should I wait for the good just to come?

Last night, this 'pleaser thing' played on my mind. Am I not the one who should be given to, as well as the one giving? What is more? I want Carla to give more to me in terms of emotions and thoughts. Physically she assists in every way. Is that sufficient? Should I not ask for more? No, she doesn't cry with me. I don't want to change her personality. I won't ask her to be someone she is not. I think my needs are right. Is it wrong to ask? In the past I have said, "I don't want to change you, but I would like to know what you think and what you feel".

On Saturday she was very irritable. I didn't know why – that was the point. And I was highly emotional. We had a disagreement about the wine and she said things to me that seemed to come out wrong.

She said, "Where do you want me to put the wine?"

I said, "I'd like those two bottles to go there."

She then wandered off into the other room.

"Where are you going?"

She said, "Just checking that there isn't space in the other room."

I said, "I could have told you that, if you'd asked."

Our tones were unpleasant and ugly. She was irritated and I was emotional. I went upstairs and had a good long cry because that's what I felt I needed to do. I was crying because I was frustrated and sad. The unpleasant tone of my voice had been a result of pure frustration. If I had been able to put the wine there myself, the argument would not have happened

Carla continued with what she was doing and then came upstairs and said, "It has been a stressful week."

I said, "It has been for me too. Why don't you talk about it?"

She said, "There's nothing to talk about."

The events of the previous two days had led up to this – my falling, keeping things to ourselves and the worry of what this all meant. The lessons to be learnt, I think, are that instead of bottling up, talk about things. If we had done this, the argument would not have happened.

While Carla was away for three or four days after my fall,

I had a conversation with her about how I felt. When I say conversation, I mean I sent an email. Although she didn't respond directly to my email, when she got back her mood and the general atmosphere was very joyous. I don't know whether that was directly related to my email, but without her saying anything she made me feel a lot better. While she had been away I had had a lot of time to contemplate. So it was good for us to have time away from each other. As we know, if someone is out of sight it makes you yearn for them all the more.

When I had my stitches out I learned that a head or face wound needs five to seven days, a torso wound seven to ten days and hands and feet about fourteen days to heal. So, like having wounded feet, it had taken me fourteen days or so to heal, to recover psychologically and emotionally from my fall. I was managing better – I think. I knew that I am loved and cared for and I drew courage from the fact that it had taken eight years from my diagnosis in 2008 to get to how I was then.

I wondered if I was a stranger in a new world? I would like to put that differently. I was a stranger in the old world before I met Carla. That and this disease took me out of that strange land that I didn't fit into. I was not who I wanted to be. I was frustrated by the way I was living. I had been unfaithful. I was not the person I wanted to be: I was sad even though I'm usually a positive person. Life then seemed unfamiliar to me. The fact of my condition complicated that, but my dream of life hadn't changed. I was happier in my new world and wanted to live life more fully. I realised that the inevitable would happen, irrespective of what one wanted. I decided that whichever way this panned out, I would live every day as best as I could. I would be happy - not solemn and sad, because that would not be good for me or for my family.

Carla

I met Kevin in 2007 when we were working at the same insurance company. From the moment we were introduced we just clicked and by the end of that year our professional relationship had become a personal one. Talk about a whirlwind romance. There we were, a new couple about to become parents. It is safe to say we were a little overwhelmed by our situation, but there was never any doubt that we were ready to commit to a life together.

As strong as our relationship was, nothing could have prepared us for the shock that was to come a few months later. That July Kevin visited a chiropractor because he had noticed a tingling sensation in his arms. He was always very active at school: he had played rugby and later became a cycling enthusiast – so he was a somewhat regular visitor to the doctor who saw to his sporting aches and pains.

During the examination the chiropractor noticed that the muscle around Kevin's thumb had lost some of its firmness. Concerned that it was a sign of reduced muscle tone, he referred Kevin to a neurosurgeon who then sent us to a neurologist. It was there that Kevin was diagnosed with Motor Neurone Disease, MND. I will never forget that moment. We sat in stunned silence with absolutely no idea of what lay ahead of us. Right from the start we made a pact that we were going to stay positive and live for each moment.

I had never heard of MND before Kevin's diagnosis, but I'm a very practical person and as I learned more about the disease I refused to see it as any kind of death sentence. MND is a progressive degenerative condition. It attacks nerve cells in the brain and spinal cord causing the body's muscles to grow weaker over time. Eventually essential activities like speech, swallowing and breathing are affected. We investigated our options, but we carried on with life – we weren't going to rush out and prepare for the worst.

At first nothing about our routine changed. Kevin continued his cycling and driving and we took things day by day. We spent a lot of time researching – the Internet makes it quite easy to find information. There is a lot of nonsense out there and more than a few moneymaking schemes, so you have to be very careful.

When Kevin started finding it difficult to drive it was time to make some changes. We lived in a double storey house so we had a stair lift installed and planned to put ramps in the garden. I bought a lounge suite for our bedroom patio for Kevin on the days that he didn't feel like coming downstairs, so he could relax and enjoy a good book in the sun. I always said that I would never allow TV in our bedroom, but as the saying goes, never say never. It's those little comforts that make the difference. When we started making plans to accommodate a full-time caregiver, my parents heard about this and offered to move in immediately. I've never been more grateful. Living with your parents after so many years is tough, but we have made it work.

We bought a car equipped for Kevin's needs and my mum drives him around in it. She helps with Kian's lunches and lifts. It's also a huge relief to have my dad around to take Kian to play soccer and ride his bike. Kian absolutely loves physical activities and we don't ever want him to feel lonely by missing out on fun with his friends. I don't think there is any professional in the world who would have cared for us in our situation as much as my parents do.

When we saw the first doctor in 2008 he gave Kevin two

to five years to live. It's now eight years later and he is still going strong. I really believe that his positive mindset is the reason for that. He decided early on that he wanted to live his life and not become a recluse. It would be so easy for him to sit in front of the TV all day, but instead, Kevin's schedule is always full. He used to visit my offices twice a week to help out with training and a mentorship program and spend another two days at physiotherapy therapy and hydrotherapy.

Every year so far we have treated ourselves to a trip overseas. We also take shorter trips throughout the year. It's quite a task, arranging special porters and hotels with the right facilities. But if you plan well, nothing is impossible. I'm determined for us to travel together while we still can. One of the biggest lessons I've learnt is the importance of spending time with those you love, and those who love you. On most weekends there are impromptu dinners and quality time spent with family and friends – people are surprised about how well and how much we get out.

In our house we each have our own hobbies. Kevin stopped working and started buying wine. He just loves it. Sometimes our house looks like a winery stacked wall-to-wall with boxes. The garage is jam-packed too. He really enjoys the research which is a necessary part of being a successful wine collector.

I found my hobby and exercise – I ran a half marathon earlier this year and I'm training for a cycle race. I promised myself that I would find time for me outside of work, Kian and Kevin. I train twice a week in the early morning, either with a spinning class or a run. I leave before everyone else is awake and I'm back in the house by 6 am. I also love Pilates and take classes twice a week with friends. I would never have thought that I would become an exerciser but it helps me clear my mind, and I recommend it to anyone.

But every day is not perfect, I must admit. We both have moments when things become too much. Kevin has been seeing a psychologist since he was diagnosed, which is very helpful. Sometimes you just need a different perspective on your situation and gain insight from someone else who isn't right in the middle. We are not embarrassed to admit that we've sought help. Sometimes Kevin is brought to tears by his frustration, especially when he discovers something new that he is no longer able to do. And there are mornings when I have to compose myself in the car before I head to work. It's normal, though, and it's healthy to remember that if you need to have a moment it is right to go ahead and take it. We don't ignore our feelings as long as we can share what we're thinking. I know it will be fine.

We choose to live for the special moments like Tuesday evenings which are just for Kevin and me. We don't go out. We just open a bottle of wine and watch a movie. And then there is my favourite time of the day when our son Kian climbs into our bed for a cuddle.

Moments that we – Kevin and I cherish.

Sidelines

Viv took me to see Deon Nel. He has MND. I felt very comfortable with him. Deon has one of those contraptions that pick up eye movements on the computer screen and help you read. On the way back, Viv started a discussion about whether one wants to 'live like that'. It didn't distress me, it irritated me even though I understand that that is the way she feels. I can't make a decision at the moment about how I want to live, and nor should she as she is not in my position. The fact that my decision may be creating a burden on my family is what I have to think about. My irritation with Viv was my sense that perhaps she believes I should feel as she does. While the future does scare me, my fears may be different from those of other people I have met. I enjoy having interaction with others with MND and feel that I am able to be positive. I have always wanted to be a giver and it is rewarding, even though it might only be my time that I'm giving.

I have often felt that I am in a box with a label. This label affects people I meet very differently, as things have changed from my being able to do everything for myself and my family, to my not really being able to do anything physical at all. One of my greatest challenges is to accept that I have very little control over the present and none at all over the future. To be able to manage that knowledge, and to understand what it really means, has demanded that I change my attitude – to everything. You cannot imagine how big everything is – and that's just thinking about the things I used to take for granted: scratching my ear, eating my breakfast, turning over in bed.

My sons Luke, Joel and Kian are getting on with their lives, as I watch from the side-lines. Carla has a busy and demanding work life – a life I used to share with her. And that too I watch from the side-lines. It used to upset me terribly when I couldn't get to watch Joel, Luke and Kian on sports days or at matches, or when Carla had to go away on business trips. All these I had control over and could be there and enjoy whenever I wanted to. I still want to. That hasn't changed at all. Being angry at not being there is no longer my response. Sadness – yes I feel that in great big heavy chunks.

What would life be without hope? It's easy for healthy people to say things like "I don't want to live if I am on a respirator and fed through a tube". Now, as one who is deteriorating, I rebel against death and I choose hope and life. I want to see my sons grow up. I want them to have a dad who loves then and provides as best as he can for their physical and emotional well-being. To show and tell them that life is full of choices, and that it is always possible to make the positive choice. To be able to choose how you live your life within your circumstance. To remain positive is my choice.

I'd so love to be able to take some of Carla's burden – take Kian to the doctor, go with her to Monte Carlo on her business trip. Her boss did ask if I'd like to go and I was so torn. I wanted to be there to support Carla, and just to be with her but it would have been a hectic business, and I'd have had to pay for a carer to help me. So, much as I missed her, it made far better sense to spend the money on a family holiday.

Which we did. We went to Mabalingwe. Carla wanted to take Kian on a drive to see the lions in an open 4x4. I did so want to go with them and to do memorable stuff with my family. But it would have been almost impossible for me to climb up into the vehicle. So I watched them drive off without me.

Sidelined! That is what this MND does. You lose out.

Do I have a choice?

Do I want to live like that?

At the moment I want to live, no matter what. I never really expected to be cured, but I do believe that the longer I live, the more there is a chance that a cure may be found. So the object is to give myself the opportunity of being cured by living as long as possible. If, for example, there is a cure in fifteen years' time I could be cured and still be within the three score and ten allotted years.

A friend sent me this verse:

So we're not giving up. How could we? Even though on the outside it often looks like things are falling apart on us, on the inside, where God is making new life, not a day goes by without His unfolding grace. These hard times are small potatoes compared to the coming good times, the lavish celebration prepared for us. There's far more here than meets the eye. The things we see now are here today, gone tomorrow. But the things we can't see now will last forever.

2 Corinthians 4:16-18 MSG

Looking Back

There have been major events in my life. Some I don't personally remember: they have been retold but I sense they too have been defining moments. I wonder: if I did not have to manage and somehow survive MND, would I even be considering those events in my present context.

I was a year old and in hospital with pneumonia, and according to my mom it was touch and go whether or not she would ever see me again. She told me how she had to drive to hospital alone in Port Elizabeth. It was a strange city to her because we were visiting my grandparents. My grandparents and my dad were more pragmatic and practical, and said that they wouldn't visit as they felt I would not know they were there. I don't agree. I believe that no matter what the situation, one is always aware of the presence of others.

Although I don't remember it, my will to survive that life-threatening illness was a turning point. Now, no matter what my situation, I won't give up. That is a big part of me as I face MND. I won't give up and call it a day. As an adult I feel the emotion my mom must have had then when she had to think that her baby could die. As a parent I now understand her desperation. This brings me to the time when Joel was critically ill with meningitis. His situation was similar to mine when I had pneumonia, but he had the will to survive. There is a great similarity in Joel's and my character.

∼

Joel's illness was the turning point in my marriage to Valerie, my childhood sweetheart. Joel's illness was a frantic experience for both of us. Valerie seemed to think that I was not as worried and concerned about Joel as I should have been, and thought that her emotions and anxiety were more important than mine. My mom had come to stay with us while Joel was sick.

One night while Joel was still in hospital my mom made toast for Valerie when she came home from work but Valerie didn't like it because it was a bit burnt. Nothing was said until the following morning when Valerie and I argued about the meal. We were both upset and Valerie wanted to get to Joel in hospital and wouldn't finish the conversation. I went outside and stood in front of the car. She nearly ran me over in pure rage. That was the moment I realized that our marriage couldn't continue as it was.

I was upset and disappointed: I felt she did not value my life. That event was a very important turning point for me. Added to this was the thought of losing Joel. I still feel very emotional when I think about it.

I had to consider all the implications of what had happened that morning. Things had not been good between us and I'd been having an affair for a while. This was a symptom of my unhappiness and it compounded the deterioration in our marriage.

A few months later, after much soul searching, I decided to tell Valerie about my affair. I no longer felt guilty just sad. The greatest sadness was that Luke and Joel would grow up without their mom and dad as a family. I made a decision from then on to make serious changes in my life and to live my life more honestly, both with myself and others.

I am very sorry that I wasn't honest with Valerie or myself right before we got married. I was not ready to marry her or anyone else for that matter. This was because I wasn't sure of how I wanted to live my life. I was still discovering myself: who I was and what I really wanted. I should have been man enough to say I wasn't ready, and if she didn't want to wait that we needed to forego our relationship. I didn't love or care for her as a husband should because I didn't know how. Deep inside me I knew it wasn't the right time. Throughout our marriage I wasn't really happy; I always felt a kind of vague discontent.

I can't blame Valerie for my unhappiness. I felt I wanted things from life that Valerie and I didn't have. My ideas on life were different from hers. My views were different from hers. Finances, the décor of our house, friends and friendships – we never agreed. My friends never sat well with Valerie and because of that I didn't have many. Again I can't blame her for that entirely because I had decided that, rather than create conflict, I would just not have friends.

My not speaking up earlier in our relationship was dishonest. Even though Valerie says she has forgiven me, I still think about the wrong I've done. I always loved her but I could not see us as a couple forever. What wanted from life was so different that no amount of love would have made us happy. It's about what we wanted from life. Love and hate are so close. I wanted and still want to be loved for who I am, and I didn't ever feel that I was simply loved by Valerie. I always felt that she expected and wanted more from me than I was able to do or give. In some ways I knew that she loved me, but it was conditional love, always on her terms.

After I had told her about my affair, she tried to and needed to control my thoughts and actions. This pushed me away. She would not take any responsibility for where we were in our marriage. We went to see a counsellor, but as soon as the counsellor disagreed or confronted her, she copped out. Her idea was that I should report my every movement to her and was not willing to give me the space to decide what I really wanted. She was rigid and there was no negotiation at any point. So I went away.

If Valerie had been more forgiving and less rigid, we might still have been married. Valerie seemed always to be right and everyone else was wrong. I want Valerie, and especially the children, to know that they were created out of love and not by accident. The reason things didn't work out was because my needs were not the same as hers. Valerie and I did not think the same, I was submissive in the relationship and I often allowed her needs to take priority over mine. I spent most of our time together trying to make her happy.

Consider this riddle from Jim Daly's blog:

'Everybody wants it. But if you use it in your marriage,

you could lose everything. What is it?'

The answer is control. Whether it's the right sweetener for our coffee or keeping our home at a certain temperature, we all want our life to function in a way that suits us. What do we do when something doesn't work the way we like? We try to control it, of course. Controlling behaviour can often occur because one spouse doesn't feel loved and validated by the other, so they try to control their spouse's actions to ensure they get the relationship they want. But taking charge over a spouse doesn't foster connection and love. Instead, it destroys it because control erodes partnerships and oneness, the very foundation God designed for the marital relationship.

I learned the hard truth: If you control your spouse, you're in danger of losing your marriage. In many cases, a spouse who feels controlled will try to escape. That may be through an affair, a divorce, or, at the very least, spending all of their time with friends, even in another part of the house, or going away on extended business trips. There are hundreds of other reasons.

The solution is to give up the role of 'boss' and to begin cultivating a relationship of warmth and openness.

Consider each other as equals. It may take the help of a counsellor, but when a couple learns healthy ways to connect and become complimentary in the way God intended, a strong marriage is just over the horizon.

Nothing to Lose

The beginning of school at Barberton Primary was very important for me. I still think about it. I think about the fact that my mom was not able to be there on my first day, nor was my dad. Susan had cut her mouth the night before and had to be taken to the doctor first thing in the morning – my first day at school. I think that incident influenced the rest of life.

I guess I was about six years old. I can't remember how I felt. I don't even know what emotions I experienced then. It was really just a case of doing what I had to do – go to school on my own. I knew I was alone and I took it in my stride. I realized that I needed to do it, and that everything would not always be easy. I think I felt confident enough to face my first day of school alone because Trevor and I had been encouraged to be responsible for ourselves from the time we were very little guys. Little did I know then how this gift my folks had given us would help me in the future.

∾

Years later after Valerie and I had separated she decided to move from Johannesburg to Durban with my sons, Luke and Joel. One day she simply said, "I'm moving to Durban". No discussion. Early on that morning when she took away my access to my children, I went to say goodbye to them. The boys didn't understand. They were tearful and I was in tears. As they drove away I sobbed and sobbed.

I used to drive to Durban every second weekend to be with Luke and Joel. Then, after I had been diagnosed with MND in 2008, and I wasn't able to drive any more, I used to fly. The most difficult and saddest aspect of my incapacity is that I am not part of my two boys' daily lives and can't pick up them up from school, watch them play sports, and, especially, I can't be there to give them emotional and physical support. It's not Valarie's fault that I have MND. But I am angry with her for her taking my children away. And I am angry with her for not realizing that taking them away has had a negative impact on them psychologically, emotionally and at school. It has taken me a lot of hard work to acquire the emotional skills and tools to deal with the fact that I am not an active part of Luke's and Joel's lives. The day-to-day activities and responsibilities are not mine, and I have to trust that she will do the best she can, even though it might not necessarily be the way I'd like it to be.

∼

As I grew older, and particularly when I was a teenager, I was very insecure about myself in company. It was the Achilles heel of my teen years. Even though confidence deserted me when I was with friends, peers and teachers, I maintained my independent nature. Only after I had entered the insurance industry did I develop a little more confidence in speaking to people. Everyone has issues. Some see psychiatric and emotional help as weakness, but seeking emotional help is not the same as going to the doctor when you are sick. I believe that psychiatry can help to improve your physical and mental health.

∼

Probably my most significant life event has been my being diagnosed with MND. It has made me realize how precious life is and how fortunate I am to be able to do the things I have done and still can do with my life. I also realize how lucky I am to have Carla in my life. She is very positive and supportive. We had only been a couple for about 8 months when I was diagnosed with MND.

In a strange way MND has relieved me of a lot of burdens. When I say I am burdened, I mean my insecurities and lack of confidence. An example is the ability to be able to stand up in front of a room full of people or to be able to be assertive in a disagreement. As I've said, I used to be fairly shy and didn't have confidence in my abilities; I'd shy away if there was any confrontation. With my diagnosis of MND that suddenly seemed to disappear and I felt able to voice my opinions and make myself heard.

This confidence has extended to work and in my personal relationships. I often ponder 'why'? I then go back to the thought of being 'lucky to be alive'. It's as if a switch in my brain went on or off. I think it was a combination of Carla and having MND that helped me to change my life.

Life is too short. I suddenly felt as if I had nothing to lose.

If I was to live the statistical three to five years of someone with MND, I felt I didn't want to live the way I had been – lacking confidence and shying away. I had always wanted to make a difference in my children's lives. If I only had three to five years I had to make sure they'd know that I cared about them. Knowing that there was a possibility that I would not see out their school lives, I needed to make sure that they were looked after. I needed to say and do the things I wanted to quickly. I might not have another thirty years.

I went to see a psychologist, Dr Di Shand, but Carla didn't like her. Carla went with me for a couple of sessions. She felt that Di came across as a hard and uncompromising woman. I had chosen her because she had experience of working with both children and adults. I felt that I'd be able to speak about the issues of my children. I had my last session in January 2011 and will go back if necessary. However, Carla doesn't like psychology: she is a strong woman and can deal with 'stuff' herself. I don't think she needs to see a psychologist now, although she might have to deal with some issues later. On the other hand, I tend to get emotional about things. Carla and I have an arrangement. Because I tend to cry when I get upset or angry, I write to her... "Hello My Love..."

Rugby and Me

My first rugby game I ever watched was with my dad on TV: Transvaal against Western Province. The next one I remember watching was the All Blacks against South Africa in 1981. I must have been eight or nine years old. After seeing those games all I wanted to do was play rugby. My mom took me to rugby practice in Barberton once or twice a week. I played eighth man. When I got home from school all I wanted to do was to kick the ball around. And it was my mom who played rugby with me. I was not pushed by my parents but we were always encouraged to do what I we enjoyed. Rugby was my passion.

We moved from Barberton to Graskop and I went from a big school with many students to a small school with only one Under-13 rugby team. When I was in Standard

3 (Grade 5) I tackled a big bloke in Standard 5 (Grade 7). He was quite impressed. I was quite light and so played mostly on the wing. The next year I played in the scrum as hooker even though I wasn't big. What I enjoyed best was tackling not actually running with the ball although I was good at that too.

Trevor and I played Running Red Rover and Open Gate together at break with the other chaps, and continued when we got home. That was where I fell and broke a tooth. At Graskop we played against other schools. We even played against Skukuza School in the Kruger Park, barefoot among the paper thorns and the deviltjies. I remember once cutting my foot on glass, but that didn't stop me playing – I just wore a sock.

When we moved to Umtata the Under-13 rugby coach looked at me and asked me what position at played. I told him, "Hooker". He looked me up and down and at my small size and said, "You won't play hooker here." I eventually played Under-13 at full back. I seldom touched the ball, but I tackled a lot, which is what I really liked. In Umtata we had to wear boots - it was the first time I'd played rugby in boots.

In high school, I tried to get into the Under-15 team before the first match of the year. I didn't make the team. I was very disappointed and upset because I wasn't even on the bench. The guys went off to play and got severely thumped. The next weekend I was in the team and played every match after that. In my second year at high school I played Under-15. I was one of the more talented chaps in the team. Even though I was under 15, there was talk of my playing in the first team. I could have gone from the Under-15 to the Under-19 rugby team, but the headmaster decided against it. Even though there was a lot of competition, I was determined and made the first team the following year, and I did.

In the three years I played in the first team, I missed only one game. Playing in the Border Schools trials, I went to kick the ball and missed. Instead of the kicking the ball, I connected with the boot of an opposition player. I had this massive haematoma on my shin, which meant I couldn't play the next game.

I enjoyed cricket and athletics, but rugby was my favourite. Other than the physical contact in the tackling that I enjoyed, I seriously loved the team spirit part of playing rugby – the camaraderie, the friendships, and playing with chaps to achieve a common goal. I had many accolades, but my greatest enjoyment was playing – that was my passion.

After passing matric in Umtata, I played for the Collegians Rugby Club. Some of the boys' fathers whom I had called 'Oom' when I was at school were now my team mates, and we were on first name terms. It was quite an adjustment.

When I moved to Port Elizabeth Tech. I played for three teams: the Crusaders Under-21A during the week, Crusaders Under-23 team on a Friday night and the Crusaders Second open men's team on a Saturday in any of these positions: centre, wing or full-back. I didn't really enjoy my time in Port Elizabeth. The team players changed every week and as I hadn't been to one of the top rugby schools in the Eastern Province like Grey, Dale, Queens or Kingswood, I was often overlooked.

Half way through that year I went back to Umtata and battled to get back into a team. We were promoted to the Premier League in the Border region. Our first and only game was against Winter Rose whom we played at the Basil Kenyon Stadium in East London. Then the Transkei Independent Rugby Union was formed and that opened a whole new world. There were many guys playing rugby for various clubs, so we combined with other Transkei rugby teams.

The South African Rugby Union (SARU) gave Transkei rugby provincial status because they were trying to develop non-white rugby by establishing development teams. I was respected as a player, although we didn't ever win a game, but I really wanted to play serious rugby, so I joined the Old Selbornians Club in East London. I used to drive from Umtata to East London once a week for practice and once a week for a game - a round trip of 460km each time – such was my passion.

When we moved to Cape Town I played a bit of rugby on a social basis, but then it got too cold and miserable to play. I was working long hours and it was difficult to maintain my fitness. I gave up rugby and started cycling. I love cycling, I love the mountains, but I did miss the camaraderie and team spirit of rugby.

Rugby is very much part of my life and who I am - not especially because of my achievements, but because I loved the camaraderie, and what we were trying to achieve as a community. The day I decided to quit wasn't sad. I'd made a conscious decision to focus on my career once I found out who I was and what I wanted to do. I enjoyed insurance broking and was good at it. Insurance broking is much like a team sport – the same objectives apply: a team of individuals all work towards a common goal, just as rugby players do.

Hello My Love

August 2013

Hi ml

I don't know where to start. There's so much on my mind and in my heart. The past two Sundays at church have given me so much to think about. The thoughts and feelings had been there before then, but it has given me some insight.

You are the woman of my dreams. I love you with all my heart and can't imagine life without you. I appreciate everything you do for me. I mean everything. I respect you and I'm proud of you. I often can't understand why you can't see your own achievements and bask in your own glory. You are beautiful and attractive. And again I can't understand why you can't see that. It's as if what you've done, what you've achieved and who you are just not enough.

I, on the other hand, am in a situation where I am going backwards. I feel that you need me less and less. I offer very little support. The support I can offer is thought and emotion, but it feels as if you don't really need that from me. We don't really talk anymore. I mean talking about what's deep inside and not about the day's activities. I really don't know how you feel and I doubt if you know how I truly feel.

Without being able to show my affection physically, all I can do is talk. However, I would like it to be reciprocated. I know you love me, I have no doubt. It's not about love but more about how I make you feel and how I contribute to your life. It's also about my knowing how I make you feel and knowing whether you appreciate what I do.

I like affection. I like holding you and I like to be held. I like kissing and kissing passionately. I like to be close to you. Sometimes all I want to do is snuggle. I wish I could do these things without having to ask you. I wish it could be the way it used to be.

I am sad, angry, irritated, frustrated, happy, and ecstatic, all in a day – in an hour. In one moment I'm so happy and ecstatic to have you in my life, the next moment I get frustrated that I can't hug and kiss you. I am sad knowing that someday I'll not be able to kiss you passionately, tell you how I feel, make love to you, and then I am irritated because you can't see it, can't see that time is ticking away.

In terms of bucket lists this is what I'd like most: I want to share thoughts, feelings, emotions and affection with you, often. Right now I don't know whether I'm doing the right thing, whether I'm burdening you further, whether my expectations are unrealistic, whether I'm being unfair. I am scared that if I don't say this I'll regret it one day. As it is I have regrets.

I am sorry that I've not spoken to you before; my emotions get the better of me. I hope you can understand.

I love you with all my heart.

So these three things continue: faith, hope, and love. And the greatest of these is love.

(1 Corinthians 13:13)

Choices

I'd been looking at the Oscar Pistorius trial a little bit – not much. I think he had an incredibly traumatic childhood, possibly resulting in his general anxiety disorder. In spite of that, I don't think that we can go through life blaming our parents for our present situations. We are all products of the decisions we've made. I think that's very, very true. Every situation where you need to make a decision is preparation for your next decision. So each decision is a determining event – no matter how small it may seem.

I think of my boys, Luke and Joel. They've been put in a position where they spend the majority of their time with their mom. In spite of that, and because of that, they can still choose how to live their lives. I wonder what would happen if they changed their minds when they were older and wanted to come and live with me.

What about all these kids that live in the squatter camps? They are expected to behave in a way that's okay, in spite of everything. I sometimes think I'd like to take my boys into a squatter camp for them to see how privileged they really are. They've never been exposed to that level of poverty and can't imagine it or describe it.

Living on the plantation as we did, we were exposed to very, very poor black kids. We used to play with them, go into their house, and eat their food. The walls were black with soot. There was no running water. Some of them had a long drop but others didn't – they just squatted in the bush. Young as I was, it made me realize how lucky I was and how unfair life can be.

A while back Kian wanted to know when we had bought our first iPad. It made me think. He has grown up with every possible device and facility. Lots of kids don't play outside, climb trees, ride horses or swim anymore, unless their parents make a point of creating opportunities for their children, as we have with Kian. He does gymnastics, soccer and swimming and now is keen on hockey as well. Compared with Kian many other kids do nothing.

All sports are available at Luke and Joel's school. Luke likes soccer because he's not comfortable with contact sports. Joel is not too keen on sport at all. It may be that it's a lack of influence, although Valerie was also sporty, she used to play hockey, and do athletics and I think she still swims. Fortunately Luke and Joel go to after-care where they can play sport. I think it is about being encouraged and I'd like to be able to do that for Luke and Joel as well. With my encouragement Luke has started to play soccer.

I called Kian, and he stubbed his toe on the way to me. He then went on to blame me for his stubbing his toe. I asked him if I was in charge of his legs. He said no. So I asked him why he'd blamed me. Because I called him over he said. I then explained that even though I'd called him, I had no control over how he walked.

Over the past few days I'd been pondering the thought of CHOICE. I'm not a psychologist. I am merely sharing some food for thought. I have MND, I didn't choose to have it. I just got it. I can't blame anyone or anything. It is God's will. Am I angry with God? Nope. He has a plan for me. I'm still trying to figure it out.

The way I respond to the effects and consequences of MND is my choice. It is an unfortunate situation I find myself in. I'm sure we have all found ourselves in some situations that are traumatic and stressful. No one can control my choices other than me. I can't be forced to be happy or sad or angry or negative or positive or sulky or go to physio or visit a psychologist or eat a meal. My situation with MND is one of many situations I face during the course of a day. I get sad reading a story Luke wrote about me. I laugh at Kian's thoughts and response. I envy Joel's resilience. I am happy when Carla arrives home from work. I get excited about seeing my friends this weekend. I get irritated by the inconsiderate action of able-bodied people parking in disability bays.

I'm sure we all experience these emotions. It is however, the way we react to these, that is in our control. Some of you may say that one's past, past experiences and genetics will influence one's reaction or response. I agree that our natural response could be influenced by these factors. However, if I takes a moment to think before reacting. How would or should I respond? I have time to reflect and consider what the right thing to do or say is. I think about the repercussions of my actions and words. If I do this, I have no reason to blame anyone or anything else for my actions or words. As it is I should not be blaming anything or anyone. This is a moment for me to make a CHOICE. I have the power to do this. I am are in charge of myself.

God gave us all a brain, He gave us emotions. He gave us the ability to choose. There are people who sadly don't have the mental capacity to fulfil some or all of these due to disease or accident. However, for the majority of us, the one thing no one can take away from us is CHOICE.

Think about the power of choice

So next time you think about blaming something or someone for what has happened to you, think of all the choices you made up to that point and ask yourself who was in control of those choices. You may not have chosen your situation (like where you were born, where you grew up, whether your parents were divorced or wealthy or poor, or whether you were in an accident or criminal act against you or MND), but you still had and still have a CHOICE on how you going to deal with the situation. Are you going to let the situation control you or are you going to do something about it? What is your next choice going to be? You have the ability to choose. But remember for every choice made there are consequences and further choices to be made.

In our country, we are so focused on choices made by a generation half a century ago, and choices made by our present leaders. These all seem to have a negative impact on all of us. Don't you think that a positive and more loving Choice, by everyone, in our actions towards each other might just be what we need to make our country a better one?

Looking Inward

Have I become more spiritual since I was diagnosed with MND? When I was younger, my mom tells me, I wanted to be a minister in church. I think I'm the most spiritual of all our family. I read the Bible as a little boy. When Kian was born and even a bit before that Carla and I spoke about going to church and taking Kian. When we lived on the West Rand we went to church every Sunday.

When we moved to Olivedale it took a while to find a suitable church. I always wanted to have a spiritual life and I read the Bible regularly. I think I have become more spiritually in touch because the services at the New Life Church are more theme-orientated and are applied to everyday life. The minister preaches about things that you can do in life. I think I've definitely become more spiritual and I believe that my children should have some form of spiritual grounding. Luke and Joel do go to church with us when they visit me.

Without doubt the spiritual side of my life has helped me become more settled in my situation. I feel good most Sundays after church. A story about a concentration camp: a father went to work and left the mother and his son and daughter. When he came back from work he asked his daughter where her brother and mother were. His daughter told him that when they had come to take her brother away, and her mother had gone with him because he was scared. Mothers will do anything for their children. I think I might have been angry with my mom for not doing something about her situation. But in retrospect, I understand it. She was looking after us – Trevor, Susan and me. That's why she stayed to make sure that we were all cared for.

I realize that with MND I'm more aware of the world – not just the physical world, but the emotional and spiritual world as well. My senses are heightened. I've become more aware of when Carla is on edge. I leave it and keep things superficial. I feel positive because I've done the work on myself and haven't expected others to change. I used to get very anxious when Carla went away because she does a lot for me, but also because I would miss her. I don't have the same anxiety any more. I think it's related to trust.

As far as church is concerned – what Jesus Christ gave he gave without expectation. He gave unconditionally. The Bible talks about love and giving, but I don't think that is part of human nature. I've tried to love instead of hate, to give rather than take. I have less anger and fewer expectations. People often give without expectation. I have made a huge effort to reduce my anxiety, especially when it concerns others.

Baptism was on my mind for most of 2014. I was baptized as a baby, but I had a deep conviction that I needed to and wanted to be baptized again as a declaration of my deep love for Jesus. I also wanted to show my gratitude for His suffering for me and the forgiveness of sin and the guarantee of everlasting life.

It was a deeply emotional experience. I spoke to the minister who said it would be fine; Carla was also cool with it, which pleased me. I wore a pair of shorts and a t-shirt and some guys from the church helped me. It was an immersion baptism. I felt very close to God and felt that I could speak to Him as a physical person. It was a very uplifting experience that has made me feel much more at peace with things – more accepting. God will have to work very hard to get me off this physical planet. I feel I still have too much to do. I am not going to give up.

I was talking to a woman who works for the Children

with Cancer association. She'd lost her 7-year-old son to cancer about four years before. She asked me if I was ever angry with God. She felt it was OK to be angry with Him as long as we talked to Him about it. In a way I am angry because this MND is unfair to Carla and my sons.

God put me on earth to do something, and I've been trying to learn what it is. I don't feel pressure. I think it will be something I do for others with no reward for me. I'm very conscious of everything in life and that everything has certain benefits.

I was invited and privileged to talk to a group of young boys and girls at the Gibbs Leadership conference. I felt it was important for them to know and understand that leaders aren't all famous people. After the talk, as we were chatting informally, one young chap said that the talk had inspired him and that it was possible that my reason for being alive was to talk to them. Speaking and motivating those children was a great reward in itself. It made me feel good.

Keeping the Glass Half Full

The other day I met Leon de Beer again. He first got me thinking about writing this book. He asked how it was going. He's interested in the psychology of people with MND and any other terminal illness. He is curious about how I, for example, have maintained myself mentally, emotionally and spiritually. It got me thinking about how I have applied my own psychology to my condition.

I'm not sure whether this determination is hereditary or whether it's something that I've had to work on. I think that I might have had the basic qualities: the will and strength never to give up. But getting to where I am now has been incredibly hard work. Every situation demands a greater level of effort from me than ever before. I have always been able to do everything I wanted to. Some of those have stretched me physically as well as intellectually and often emotionally. Even as a child I always had a positive attitude, but I'd be disappointed and very often devastated if I lost something. I'd feel broken-hearted for days, but my approach eventually would be to ask, "What can I take from this experience and how do I move on?" I think I've approached MND in this way.

I have had to accept that I have this progressive degenerative disease; one that constantly takes things away from me. I lose things. This is not because I am careless, uncaring, or unconcerned. This is what the disease does. It takes away, has taken away and continues to take away my ability to have spontaneous, physical contact with the people I love. I have often wondered which of all the things I've had to address has been the hardest. They are all hard.

Acceptance is what I have to face each minute of every day and night. No matter what I want or need to do, I have to accept that I can't just do it. It requires planning and another person to do it for me. So, no matter how exhausted I am or how exhausted the world around me is, I have to apply my mind to be able to 'do'. I have to tame my emotions. I have always cried a lot, but now I could cry all the time. To be able to work with this MND I have to accept my situation and try to be objective about myself. I know that my weakest characteristic has always been that I am emotional and I find it difficult to say "No" to people. In addition, I'm not confrontational, and I wish I had the courage to be more aggressive.

My office has given me facilities and a place to work in, but even so, I have to accept in good faith that people need to accommodate me.

The only independent movement I can manage at the moment is to operate the little drive knob on my wheelchair. I can't shake hands. I can't hug a friend, my sister, my brother, my father, my mom, my lover and wife, my children. I have to rely on the people who love me for a hug, a kiss, or a touch. It's great to receive these without asking because people forget how important touching is. Even though I have lost my ability to support myself physically, I can sustain myself financially because I am still able to work as a consultant, and because of my critical financial planning skills.

I am a prisoner in my own body, and I constantly have to guard against self-pity. I often do feel sorry, not only for myself but also for Carla and my sons. Always thinking and being sad about my physical deterioration makes me feel worse but when I focus on what I still can do, I feel better. So, when I lose something or when something negative happens in my life I always have to ask myself, "What is the positive here?" but finding the answer is sometimes hard.

We went to Founders' Day at St Stithians where the vice rector of Wits, who has run the Comrades marathon a few times gave a speech. He said, "If your heart is happy, you can do anything. If your mind is clear and your heart is happy, things go well". This rang true because I know that my psychological outlook and state of mind have a direct effect on my physical well-being. A negative outlook on everything makes me feel worse. I've also become more aware of things around me, much like a blind person who uses smell, touch, and hearing to compensate for not being able to see. I have become more aware of atmosphere and can gauge how people are feeling by looking at the way they behave.

So, while I can't say that I benefit physically from having a positive outlook, I do feel good. I don't feel miserable. I try to focus on what I can still do I have a very positive attitude and am happy with my life. Looking back to when I was unhappy, I remember that I was often ill. My unhappiness increased my stress. In addition, I haven't had any serious illnesses. I have always been incredibly physically active and I think this has helped to slow down my deterioration. I think if I had been less fit I would have deteriorated more quickly. Now I go to physiotherapy and hydrotherapy regularly every week.

I was at a MND meeting where some of the group were saying they had lots of pain and muscle spasms. I'm sure that if I didn't go to physio- and hydro- and had been less fit when I was diagnosed, my deterioration would have been much faster and I would also have had pain and muscle spasms.

My parents didn't force us to do sport at all, they were more concerned that we should enjoy ourselves and do well because we enjoyed what we did. Although my dependence on Carla and Viv increases every day, I still do things: I work, I go to sports events, shop and travel. I won't let this disease run my life completely. I still do what I can, what I want to do and what I can afford.

I went to a talk at Emerald the other day, and learned that if you know what you truly want you should not focus on obstacles. This brings me back to the MND. For example, I want to take my children to Mauritius with us. Before we can go I need to ask: How do we get there? Can we afford it? Will it be wheelchair friendly? That is how I have to manage my life each day. We have to plan everything with a positive attitude, work around the irritating obstacles and don't let them get us down, and if they do, we just make a different plan to manage.

Carla went overseas for business. It's hard to say whether she enjoyed it because she is a woman of few words. It was very good for her career but she missed Kian a lot. I sent her long messages about love. She sent me "I love you too" messages. Sometime ago she said something that made me feel really good. I feel that as long as she is happy, I'm happy.

How is the sex? The very cold weather doesn't help. It also depends how busy we are, and who is visiting. Most mornings, if Carla doesn't go for a run, we have snuggle time. So now sex for me is passive and we have less sex and more affection. I can no longer explore and love Carla's beautiful body, but I feast with my eyes.

I have always been a sharing lover not a dominant taker, but because of my condition, we have both had to accommodate each other in new and different ways. This is where loving and understanding each other makes a difference. I have to be able to ask her to touch or kiss or hold me, even if I can't do the same for her. We have help and guidance for all the other stuff – physio- and hydrotherapy, motivational talks, support groups, spiritual advice, but nothing for sex.

MND has been a great taker-away.

I had a message via Facebook the other day. There's a couple where the wife has MND, but they have never talked about it. Carla and I do talk, and although Carla often avoids the difficult subjects, we do eventually reach an understanding. It is difficult enough when both partners in a relationship are physically able, but when one partner is disabled it is even worse.

At times I have felt that Carla has not cared about me. I

know this is not true. I was just feeling sorry for myself. I think. Carla's past relationships took their toll on her emotionally and physically, but they made her a stronger person. I think she tries to protect herself. When Kian was conceived she was over the moon. I said I wanted to be involved, but Carla said I didn't need to if I didn't want to. All the same, we both knew that we would be together for a long time. For Carla, it was a perfect moment.

All was well until I was diagnosed with MND. When I told her she said that we would get through it together. She committed herself although she knew things would get worse.

When do I call it a day? Do I ever call it a day? When I can't communicate? When I'm on a breathing machine, moving only my eyes? Could I manage that for two years? Maybe twenty years? I don't think so.

Laura and John

Mom and Dad

To this day I remember the moment I learnt that Kevin had been diagnosed with Motor Neurone disease. My first reaction was one of denial, it just could not be true, it could not be happening to him, I thought. Afterwards I wondered if I could have been the cause, if I could have done something wrong when I was pregnant with him or when he was a baby. Next, I wanted to take the hurt away from him, questioning why it was happening to him and not rather to me. I am old, he is in the prime of his life, he had just started a relationship with a wonderful woman he adored, he had two young sons who needed him and he enjoyed the job he had.

Having known somebody who suffered from Motor Neurone Disease, I knew what a debilitating disease it is.

Remembering the perfect little baby, growing into an energetic, athletic boy who turned into a splendid rugby player who loved the game, I could not visualise him as a helpless invalid. We were proud of him, not only because of his prowess on the sports field and his leadership abilities, but also because of his character. He was and is, sincere, always unbiased and the gentlest of our three children.

Our day-to-day life has not changed much since that awful day we heard, thanks to Viv, Ian and Carla who take care of Kevin. We are extremely grateful to them, especially to Carla who stands by him, and Viv who does all the things for him that I, as his mother, should be doing and would like to do. We are available at any time we are needed, and occasionally we are given the opportunity to assist. Emotionally it has affected us, his parents, more. It has brought us closer together, relying on one another for comfort. Kevin's admirable attitude and determination to make the most of a bad situation is an inspiration to us. Kevin has taught me many things, and his faith has strengthened my belief in God. We now look at life differently and appreciate what is important and meaningful, and ignore petty things. We are more sympathetic to other peoples' hardships, aware that other families also suffer heartaches.

Luke

My first born son

24 February 2016

Someone that I admire

My dad's name is, Kevin Jordan, and he lives in Johannesburg. So we fly on a plane every month to go and see him, and our parents are divorced so I hardly see him. My dad is bald and I don't want to go bald. He is a caring person he looks after Kian(half brother to me.)When we do come he takes us to places around Joburg. In my mind, I think he is a good person he also goes to church. ✓ lovely! ☺

There is a reason that he does not fly to Durban, it's because he has a disease called M.N.D which eats away his muscles. So It is very difficult for him I'm so sorry to fly to Durban(he comes once a year.) Let me tell you more about M.N.D. with my dad, he has to sit in a wheelchair because he can't walk, and his speech is going, but he has a computer that he can use his eyesight to type. He has lived with these disease for seven years and most people live with M.N.D for 3-5 years. He is putting in a lot strength and determination to see my brother and I finish Highschool, which means he has to live for nine years which is nearly double the time an average suffer lives for.   I'm so sad!!

Even with this disease, he is joyful. He encourages us to do more. It's sad, because he never plays with

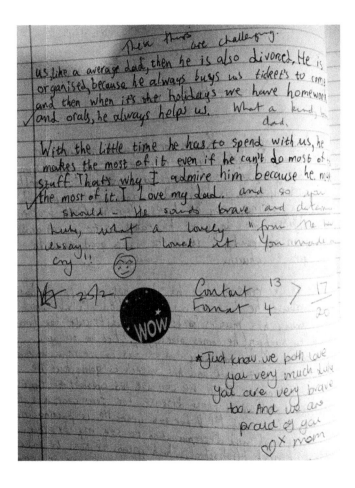

then those are challenging.
us like a average dad, then he is also divorced. He is
organised, because he always buys us tickets to come
and then when it's the holidays we have homework
and orals, he always helps us. What a kind of
dad.

With the little time he has to spend with us, he
makes the most of it even if he can't do most of
stuff That's why I admire him because he may
the most of it. I Love my dad. and so you
should — He sounds brave and deter...
luke, what a lovely " from me too
essay. I loved it. You made me
cry!! 😊

✓ 25/2   Contact 13 > 17
              Format 4   20

WOW

★ Just know we both love
  you very much luke
  you are very brave
  too. And we are
  proud of you
  ♡ X mom

Trevor

My brother, my best friend

Kevin requested that I write a short piece of about five hundred words on how his MND diagnosis affected my life and I feel privileged that he has given me this opportunity. I cannot express what a special person Kevin is and the love and respect I have for him in five hundred words. That would take many more than 500 words. However, below is a short narration of the journey followed since the day Kevin was diagnosed with MND.

So there I was sitting on our veranda with Angela, one warm East London afternoon. At that stage we were aware that Kevin was ill but there was no definitive diagnosis and I asked him to keep us informed of any new developments with regards to any test results he received from his doctors. The moment of that call is still vivid in my memory. I broke down like I have never done before after Kevin hung up. I was very fortunate to have Angela comfort me, but she also could not contain her emotions. I cannot express the devastation that I felt and could not fathom what Kevin was going through at that point in time.

At that stage, when Kevin was diagnosed, my life was not following the direction I had planned. My business was in dire straits financially, having great difficulty with cash flow as clients were not paying us. The stress was enormous and I was feeling that life was unfair to me. Kevin's diagnosis was a massive wake-up call. It made me realise how precious life is and that one's physical health, spending time with family and friends and doing what one enjoys is far more important than any business and money making ambitions. For me, finding a balance in all of these suddenly became a priority. I gave up the business, it was liquidated. This was a life changing decision which I made purely on what I had learnt and emotionally experienced by Kevin's diagnosis.

You will see that I call Kevin my best friend. This has been the case my entire life. We were so fortunate to have each other as playmates when we were young. I remember the years at ETTC, a forestry station in Mpumalanga, where we played with toy cars in soil, played in the river that flowed past the our house, rode bicycles in the forests with absolute freedom and spent many hours together playing Lego. Then moving to Mthatha and growing up; as teenagers our paths led slightly different routes and studies after school away from home in Port Elizabeth and Durban kept us apart, but I always felt that the connection between us remained as it still does.

One thing that always makes me feel extremely happy is seeing Kevin laugh. His facial expression and nearly closed eyes when laughing from deep down in his stomach gives me a feeling of happiness that I cannot explain. Over the years we have come to realise that our sense of humour is different to most people and often the fact that people are surprised at whatever it is we are laughing at makes it even more amusing.

Kev, your positive attitude and fighting spirit is awe-inspiring. Your disease, as horrible as it is, has not stopped you from living your life to the fullest extent possible. You battle simple tasks daily and by doing so have and will always teach me about the value of life. Callen often says that you are his hero and I can see why.

Always in my thoughts,

Love you my Brother.

Susan

My sister

I am lucky. I grew up with two older brothers who are quite different yet have the same core values. Being the youngest I was always seen as spoilt and a pain to have around as I followed them everywhere. All I wanted was to be with them, my heroes. They taught me so much without even knowing they were doing so. Kevin was way more inclusive in the early years – maybe because he had already had to deal with the addition of a sibling. This is Kevin; inclusive, empathetic, considerate of others and able to share; this has always been Kevin even before MND got hold of him.

Back to the early days, the years before I was five, the years that I believe shaped me most, the years on the plantation at ETTC, near Barberton in the Eastern

Transvaal. This is where Kevin and Trevor played in the forest, built go-karts, cycled everywhere on their bikes, swung on power lines, swam in the river behind the house, and tried to ditch the little sister who followed them around all the time. Sometimes they fought as brothers with only fourteen months' age difference do. I hated this and always tried to stop the fights. I didn't want to pick sides. This is where I learnt what I believe to be my most valuable talent: to see every situation from more than one perspective.

Today, it's hard for me to sit here and think about how Kevin's diagnosis of MND has affected me. Even as MND steals Kevin's voice away, he still has valued opinions and I hold his opinion on matters in the highest regard. He once asked me when I was going to settle down and get a real job. The situation he was in at that time made him think and ask that. That situation has changed and I believe that it was not MND that changed it, it was a choice Kevin made even before he'd heard of MND. Now Kevin says that doing what makes us happy is more important than trying to fit to a mould. MND does not change us at our core – it merely changes the situation in which we find ourselves.

Unfortunately, however, MND is not a situation that we can choose to change, it is a reality that Kevin and all of us whose lives he has touched live with. The greatest effect that this disease has had on me is that I know that

Kevin will not always be there to share his wisdom and I cannot change that.

The helplessness I feel for not doing more, not knowing what to do and wanting to fix it, can be very frustrating and overwhelming. And then there is the guilt of knowing that I am not the one with MND; I am not the one undergoing this ordeal, and asking why I should feel angry and sad and helpless. I cannot imagine being in Kevin's position, no matter how good I am at seeing things from all perspectives.

Alan

My friend

Kevin is a true legend, especially the way he has accepted his illness and become an awesome ambassador for MND, along with Carla. I have never felt so proud of another man before. I put Kevin and Carla and the boys on the highest pedestal, where they belong. I cannot comprehend the challenges they face daily and overcome daily because of MND.

Kevin has always been my best friend, from way back in junior school; and through his illness I believe we have become closer. There is nothing I would not do for him and his family; I hope they know this.

Being exposed to MND has really opened my eyes. I always tried to live by the saying: 'Life is not a dress rehearsal; there is no time for could've, would've, should've'. I believe this even more so now, because none of us knows how much time we have left on earth; we don't know when illness or accident may strike. We have to value each day and each moment with those precious to us. Nicklebacks' song *If today was your last day* (https://youtube/lrXIQQ8PeRs) rings true.

On a final note, I must once again mention Kevin's LOVE, Carla. I have never seen so much love shared between two people as I see with Kevin and Carla. They are a great testimony to 'in sickness and in health'. Despite the immense challenges Carla faces in her work environment, and raising a young family, she has never wavered in her love and support for Kevin. Thank you Carla, for looking after my friend.

Making a Difference

Kevin was diagnosed with MND in 2008 and initially given two to five years to live. But from the day he was diagnosed we agreed on two things: firstly that we would take each step as it came. PEG tubes, breathing assistance and wheelchairs - we were not going to stress about things in the future that we had no control over; secondly and probably most importantly we decided that we would continue to live life, be positive and do all the things we always dreamed of doing.

When Kevin stopped working and became more and more immobile, he started attending the monthly Motor Neurone Disease Association of South Africa (MNDA) meetings, where he realized that many of the people diagnosed with MND struggle to deal not only with the emotional side of the disease, but also with the financial stress that it puts on people and their families. We also heard many horror stories of people in the rural areas who go misdiagnosed, or whose families just leave them to die as they don't know what's wrong with them, or others who have no access to the physical items like walking frames, wheelchairs, bi-pap machines that are required as the disease progresses.

As a couple we realised that although Kevin's diagnosis of MND was really horrible, we are actually the lucky ones. Kevin has a disability pension; we have medical aid; we have a supportive and loving family and group of friends. We have been privileged as there are people who are far worse off than we are. Also, although the MNDA of SA is a lovely organisation, they specialise mostly in palliative care (they are affiliated to hospice) and lending equipment as and when they have things available, but they do not have the resources to focus on fundraising and raising awareness of the disease in our country.

This is where we thought we would be able to make a difference. So, in February 2013 we launched a Facebook page and website and the initiative grew from there: in 2013 we raised R100 000 and in 2014 we managed to double it and raise R200 000 and in 2015 we raised R 125,000. We now have almost 700 followers on Facebook and we don't only host fundraising events, but we also do things to help raise awareness. We recently had more than seventy people walking for MND at the 702 Walk the Talk event and received some good radio and press coverage. We also showcased our charity at an insurance institute event earlier this year to about 400 people. Obviously it's great to raise money, and our target this year is R250 000, but more than anything we want to spread awareness of MND and the realities of living with a terminal illness. Every year we donate all the money we raise to the association.

Looking Forward

It is nearly eight years since I was diagnosed with MND, and I have been working on this book for about four of those years. It has been a journey of self-discovery, forgiveness of myself as well as love and acceptance of others. When I started this project I was full of anger, anxiety, fear and frustration. I have changed in so many ways that the anger I have felt towards others has given way to forgiveness, understanding and acceptance. My anxiety and great fear have been replaced by hope, love and spiritual fulfilment.

My fear is no longer for myself, but for the next generation, especially my children. All I can hope to do is to try to prepare them as best as I can with the love and help of their mothers, to face the challenges they will have growing up. My frustration is no longer directed at my own inability to do the things I used to do and would still love to do, but rather at society as a whole. Love and caring for others seems to be the exception rather than the rule.

Although I am able to do very little for myself now, I am at peace, and look forward to every new challenge with a smile and joy in my heart. I have so much to be grateful for.

Carla, my wonderful wife, you have supported me and have stood by me every step of the way, through the good times and the bad times. The other day, after you had helped me get into bed and I was smiling, you asked me Why and I said because I have the amazing and gorgeous you in my life. You gave me a hug and smiled back.

Luke, Joel and Kian, my wonderful sons, you are becoming more and more confident and are blessed with good intellect – I am sure that's from your mothers. And your good looks, of course, come from me. I am very proud of what you have achieved and have managed to do through some difficult times.

Viv and Ian you have been pillars of strength in your wonderful support of us as a family, beyond all expectation, especially Viv, who has been my care-giver and go-to person.

Laura and John, my parents, you are always in my thoughts. I know you would love to be closer and more involved in my life, but you are enjoying retirement the way you ought to. You spent the best part of twenty years trying to prepare me for life – I'm sure that wasn't easy, so you deserve all the rest you can get. Thank you for the freedom I enjoyed through my childhood.

Trevor, you have always been my best friend and you, Angela and your family have been supportive of me and my family for as long as I can remember.

Susan, I have got to know you more deeply, although we have been separated by thousands of miles.

Alan, you have been one my best and most constant friends. We have known each other for more than thirty years

Valerie, my childhood sweetheart, my first wife and mother of Luke and Joel, you have played an enormous part in my life.

Leon de Beer, you were the man who suggested that I write this memoir.

And to all my work colleagues and fellow rugby team friends and players who shared the joys of achievement through their dedication and hard work: you inspired me then, you inspire me today.

Rae Nash, my co-writer and editor, has been with me through the three and a half years it has taken to get this short memoir into shape. It has been time of friendship and emotional growth and change.

I love you all and thank you for the love, support and positive impact you have had on my life.

I am more spiritually fulfilled and this has helped me enormously in facing the future. We all have a purpose, no matter how obscure it may be. We all have special gifts and the challenge for me has been to identify them, nurture them and grow with them.

My journey is not over yet.

I need to fulfil my purpose.

I am dying to live.

Reflections

Trevor and I were born 14 months apart; but we grew up not just as brothers but as best friends as well. We moved to a new house at the Eastern Transvaal Timber Company Plantation. Next to the house was a rondavel with cottage pane windows. Mom and Dad thought it was a good idea to use this as a play room for us. One day Trevor was on the outside and I on the inside. We began throwing our Matchbox cars to each other through the glass panes. Once every pane was broken we burst out laughing. Mom heard us and came to see what was happening. Needless to say she was very upset. When Dad arrived home from work, we were nowhere to be seen. We had wisely decided to stay out of sight. Eventually we managed to negotiate with my Mom, who was the go between with Dad, that we would come home on condition that we were not punished.

We knew we'd been naughty. We didn't need anyone to tell us we were wrong. And you can't run from the consequences.

~

Trevor and I were about 3 or 4 years old out on our tricycles. We stopped and climbed up to a little ledge where we sat for a while. When we got down again there was a big puff-adder lying next to our tricycles. We called for Mom and she came out in her gumboots with the big spade and decapitated it.

Never be afraid to call or ask for help when you think you may be in a spot of bother. Some things are best handled by another person. Know the difference.

~

We didn't know until we were much older that Mom was very afraid of snakes.

Love can triumph over fear.

~

Our electricity was supplied by a lighting plant in the shed. It supplied the three houses in our row. There was an auto switch in my parents' bedroom to turn off the lighting plant at night. A wire ran above some boulders in the yard from the shed to our house. Trevor and I were jumping off the boulders and Trevor grabbed the wire and swung on it and it broke. This time we were less confident about Dad's response. Trevor hid away when he came home. My Mom begged me to let her know where Trevor was. Once again I managed to negotiate no punishment.

Never underestimate the power of negotiation.

∾

My first day at school in Barberton Primary was quite an event for me. The day before I was due to start Grade 1, my sister Susan had an accident and cut her mouth badly. She had to go to the doctor the next morning – that was the day my Mom was going to take me to school – to my first school on my first day. Neither my Mom nor Dad could take me. So they asked a neighbour to take me. I was the first child at school that morning. The next child to arrive was Nathanial Higginbottam. We sat on the steps and had a jolly good old chat. Living in the Plantation meeting strangers was unusual. I had been given the responsibility to be independent and I managed it and felt good.

In meeting a new person remember they may be just as afraid as you are to start a conversation. Make the first move and see how good it feels.

∾

I was in Standard 5 and there was an athletics meeting coming up. The night before I could not sleep, I was nervous and worried. The biggest thing was I was concerned about was how I'd look the next day. Especially which pair of shoes I should wear. I came from the country and the town children at the new school considered their appearances to be very important – especially girls, and the way they saw boys.

Be true to yourself. There is someone out there who will love and respect you for who you are. You are unique and different and special. Be patient.

≈

A family, also called Jordan, lived on the Plantation. Their children were a few years older than Trevor and me. We often played and rode our bikes together. One day, one of them gave me a chili to eat. I didn't know what it was. My mouth burnt so much that I drank water from a puddle. On the school bus one day the same boy gave me some aloe to eat. It was so bitter. This time I had nothing to drink.

Don't accept things at face value, don't be afraid to ask and don't automatically trust people who seem older and wiser than you.

~

At school we were all playing kissing-touches at break when the bell rang. I was so intent on chasing one of the girls, that by the time I'd caught her everybody had made the lines to go into the classroom. I got into quite serious trouble.

It may seem like fun at the time, but remember that there are consequences for all our actions.

~

Trevor was often in the wars; he was hit on the head and got concussion, he caught his toe in a bicycle chain, playing hockey he got hit on the head and had stitches. Trevor always did things with passion and still does.

If you approach life with vigour and passion, you may get hurt. Never let that stop you.

~

My parents bought some bantam chickens. They lived with the ducks' in the coop behind the house where the river ran. One day I decided that my bantam needed to learn to swim too. So I put it in a big bowl of water and ordered it, "Swim, swim, swim." Needless to say it wasn't very successful. My Mom saw me walking back to the house with a very sorry looking chicken in my hands. She took it into the kitchen, revived it with mouth-to-mouth. Then she lit the oven to warm and dry it. It recovered and survived until all the ducks and chickens were eaten by the mongoose.

All creatures, humans and others are different. Find out that difference and treat each difference with respect.

~

Although Trevor and I played a lot together we often used to fight. One day on our way to play outside we went through the kitchen. One of us upset the other and we started throwing pots and pans at each other. My uncle who was visiting called Mom and said, "Jou kinders gaan mekaar doodgooi (*Your children will throw each other dead*)." My Mom came and sorted us out.

There is often humour to be found in most situations. Make sure you find it.

~

When Trevor was still a baby I pushed his empty pram towards the bridge over the river near our house. There'd been a lot of rain, and the river was quite high. The pram ran off the road under the bridge. I was trying to stretch over the bridge to get the pram. My Mom saw me and ran as fast as she could to catch me before I fell into the river.

Loving is a responsibility. Take it seriously.

~

One day, playing in the garden, I picked up what I thought was a hose pipe; but it was a snake. I wasn't bitten but after that I was more cautious.

Situations and things are not always what they seem to be. Look carefully and be focused.

∼

Trevor and I were probably eight or nine years old and were playing Running Red Rover in the playground. At the end of the playground was a diamond mesh fence on top of which were sharp points. Trevor ran into the fence and ripped his ear. It was dangling, open and bleeding. I took him to the head's office on the other side of the playground leaving a trail of blood. My Mom was called in and took Trevor to hospital to have stitches.

In a stressful situation there's no need to panic; just do what you can and keep your cool.

∼

Luke and Joel and I went to a fun fair in Durban. Luke was 4 and Joel was 2 years old. Luke was so keen to go on this big zip line. It started at the top of an embankment. Joel was in a push chair. Luke got hooked up and went down the zip line, all smiles. When he got back I helped him out the harness. Suddenly Joel's push chair a started rolling down the embankment with Joel in it. I raced after it, but I couldn't catch up and it overturned at the bottom of the hill. Fortunately Joel only had a small graze on his leg. I burst into tears; because I was so distraught knowing that it could have been worse.

Treasure life and learn from it. It can be taken so quickly at any time. Always check the brakes.

~

At Border athletics trials I was doing long jump. My first attempt; I stepped on the line, second was good, third was an over-step, fourth was good and the last jump was the worst overstep of all. I didn't win.

Whatever you do, do it the best of your ability. It's good to win but winning is not everything. Just being there was exciting.

∿

I was in the 100 metre sprint race in matric. I had decided that my aim was to beat the fastest runner in the school. I did and was very pleased – but I felt sorry for the guy I'd beaten so I didn't want to make a big celebration of winning.

Always be humble and be kind, especially if others may be upset by your victories.

∿

Trevor and I decided to make a go-cart. My sister wasn't using her pram anymore. We knew how to use tools so we took the wheels off, added bits of wood and made ourselves the go-cart.

Don't always have to rely on others for what you want. Be resourceful. Make use of everything that is available.

∾

In my working career I have discovered that often the noisiest people often lack confidence and knowledge. One of the best people I've worked with had little to say, but what he said always had a great impact. And what he said was always said with kindness and a willingness to help.

A gentle response diffuses anger, but a sharp tongue kindles temper. Knowledge flows like spring water from the wise; fools are leaky faucets, dripping nonsense.

∾

I am often defensive and emotional if I am criticized. I am learning to take the positive out of things. That goes a long way to creating good relationships.

MND has taught me precisely this.

~

The time is now, the place is here. Stay in the present. You can do nothing to change the past, and the future will never come exactly as you plan or hope for.

It's never too late to start your life dream.

~

Life throws curved balls all the time. You only have one life, so how do you deal with these?

I see curved balls as challenges. I love challenges. Challenges are a way to live life to the fullest.

~

I would love to leave you, my sons, Luke, Joel and Kian, a legacy of self-confidence and belief in your own abilities.

Start small. Do something every day that takes you out of your comfort zone. Build on this and your self-esteem will grow.

~

Having you, my children, Luke, Joel and Kian, has changed my entire perspective of life. You are the most uplifting responsibility and experience of my life. Thinking of the moments when Luke, Joel and Kian were born fills me with so much emotion that I cry with happiness.

Each one of you is so special and I love you with all my heart. I loved you from the first moment and have continued to do so.

~

Look ahead and consider what may happen when you decide on an action and take responsibility for the outcome.

Take responsibility for your choices. No matter what your situation, you can choose how to live your life. In making these choices, take time to consider all the facts and the impact they may have.

∾

Make a clean break with all cutting, backbiting, and profane talk. Be gentle and sensitive with one another, forgive one another as quickly and thoroughly as God in Christ forgives you. Ephesians 4:26-27, 31-32 MSG

This takes practice but it is worth the effort.

∾

Life is to live your dreams.

The best day to get started on your dreams is today – not when you've solved all your problems or when you have more money in the bank. "Those days" never seem to get here. Make a list or a vision board.

～

How many of us still have dreams as we race through life?

Don't forget what you truly want from life. Hold the dream. Pursuing these dreams comes with commitment and hard work. Keep going.

～

Before I was diagnosed with MND I didn't think too much about my dreams. I had a lifetime to live these dreams. Now I've become more aware of what's important in life. My dreams aren't exactly the same either. I however have dreams and I try to live them.

If you wait for perfect conditions, you will never get anything done. No point in dreaming if you don't take action.

～

After I left Tech I was a window man for a while until I decided what I wanted to do.

Find what you are you're good at, do it, and enjoy it.

～

The weak let their circumstances determine their destiny. The strong let their commitments determine their destiny. I still do as much as I can.

I Live by this.

~

To think about your life is to create it. You have to take ownership of where you are right now and know where you want to go before you can get there. Keep collecting evidence for your success.

If you believe it, you can be it.

~

A cheerful heart brings a smile to your face; a sad heart makes it hard to get through the day. An intelligent person is always eager to take in more truth. A miserable heart means a miserable life.

A cheerful heart fills the day with song. Be a good listener. Just being there can be a comfort.

～

In every situation where you need to make a decision it will influence your next decision and the chain of events in the rest of your life.

Evaluate these decisions and commit to the good ones and don't repeat the bad ones. Every morning press the restart button.

～

So these three things continue: faith, hope, and love. And the greatest of these is love. – 1 Corinthians 13:13

Love is a commitment. Take it seriously. But know that you can never be responsible for another's happiness, although you can contribute.

∽

Links and References

Website: www.youandmevsmnd.co.za

www.facebook.com/YouandMeVersusMND

My YouTube Channel:
http://smarturl.it/KevinYouTube

Focus@JimDalyBlog.com

Maya Angelou's poetry and work

Sharp Pencils Creative Writers

Writer & editor: raewrite01@gmail.com

Obsidian Worlds Publishing: www.owpublishers.com

About the Author

Kevin is 44 years old. He has lived with Motor Neurone Disease for eight years. This is much longer than the average life expectancy of two to five years. Kevin played provincial level rugby and has been a successful insurance consultant. He is married to Carla and has three young sons. Much of his time is spent fundraising for the *MND Association of South Africa*, through his charity, *You and Me vs MND*.

Printed in Great Britain
by Amazon